Great Rivers

Contents

A River's Journey 4

Shaping the Land 6

Rivers of Life 8

People and Rivers 10

Exploring Africa 12

Great Rivers of the World 14

A Tale of Two Rivers

　The Nile River 16

　The Amazon River 18

Life Along a River 20

Using Rivers Today 22

Power from a River 24

Change with Care 26

Fun on the River 28

Glossary 30

Index 31

Discussion Starters 32

Features

Do you know that some salmon can swim thousands of miles up a river? Find out more in **A Mighty Journey** on page 8.

What amazing adventures did a British explorer have when she visited deep forests in Africa? See **Exploring Africa** on page 12.

What does the Amazon River have in common with a group of women? Turn to page 19 to find out.

Can people really clean a river that's so polluted it sometimes runs red? See **Cleaning the Connecticut** on page 27 for the full story.

What can we do to look after rivers?

Visit www.rigbyinfoquest.com
for more about RIVERS.

A River's Journey

Rivers carry the freshwater needed for life on Earth. A river usually starts high in mountains. The **source** can be an underground spring, an area with heavy rainfall, or melting snow on a mountain. As a river flows downhill, it is joined by other streams called **tributaries.** It ends at a **mouth**, where it flows into a lake or an ocean.

A river usually first tumbles down steep hills, rushing over rocks and waterfalls. As the land flattens, a river slows and winds gently through valleys and plains.

1

2

3

Rivers have three sections. The *upper course* flows quickly. The *middle course* winds along valleys. The *lower course* crawls to a lake or a sea.

1 Source
2 Upper course
3 Middle course
4 Tributary
5 Lower course
6 Mouth

The Ganges

Many people think rivers are special places. The Ganges River in India is sacred to Hindu people. Many Hindus travel from around the world to bathe in the river.

5

Shaping the Land

Running water is very powerful. Over millions of years, rivers wear down Earth's surface, carving out deep valleys and carrying away rock. When tiny pieces of rock build up around seas and lakes, plains of rich soil are formed for use as farmland.

A river can also change the land quickly. Heavy rain or melting snow can cause a river to swell and flood the surrounding land in just a few hours. Sometimes, a flood can cause a river to burst its banks and completely change direction.

Niagara Falls, North America

How Is a Waterfall Formed?

Waterfalls are formed where a fast-flowing river passes over a layer of hard rock. Softer rock downstream is worn away by the water, leaving a steep drop for the water to plunge over.

Rivers of Life

A river is home to many different plants and animals. Some, such as tiny algae and fish, live in the water. Plants grow well along a riverbank, and many kinds of animals come down to the river to drink, bathe, and feed.

Different plants and animals are found in different parts of a river. Fish such as salmon are strong swimmers that live in fast-flowing parts of the river. In slow-moving waters, plants such as water lilies grow well.

FAST FACTS

A Mighty Journey

Salmon hatch in pools near the sources of some fast-flowing rivers. They swim downstream and then out to sea but return to lay eggs in the same part of the river where they hatched. They swim upstream and across **rapids,** using their sense of smell to find "home."

Bears in Alaska and Canada are quick and strong. They can easily snatch a salmon from a fast-flowing river.

People and Rivers

For thousands of years, people have settled beside rivers. Rivers provide freshwater for drinking, cooking, and washing. The rich land along a river can be ideal for farming.

In the past, traveling by river was often the quickest and easiest way to explore new lands. Many famous explorers followed rivers. As business between towns increased, rivers became important highways for moving goods on boats and barges.

Saint Lawrence River, Canada

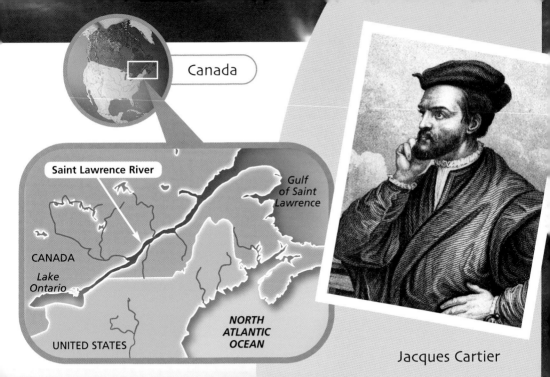

Canada

Saint Lawrence River

Gulf
of Saint
Lawrence

CANADA

Lake
Ontario

UNITED STATES

NORTH
ATLANTIC
OCEAN

Jacques Cartier

Following the River

In 1535, French explorer Jacques Cartier led a group of adventurers up the Saint Lawrence River in Canada. By the late 1700s, goods such as furs and wood were shipped down the river and then across the Atlantic Ocean. The Saint Lawrence River is still a major shipping route today.

Exploring Africa

Mary Henrietta Kingsley (1862–1900) was a British explorer. She traveled to unmapped parts of Africa in 1893 and 1894.

Not much is known about her first visit, but her second visit began at the mouth of the Ogowé River in Gabon, Africa. Mary traveled by canoe up the river to explore parts of forest not yet seen by a European. She collected insects, shells, fish, and plants for the British Museum.

In 1899, Mary left for South Africa to collect fish from the Orange River. However, she arrived in Cape Town just as a war began. She helped nurse prisoners until she caught a fever in the prison camp. She died in June 1900 and was buried at sea.

Mary Kingsley

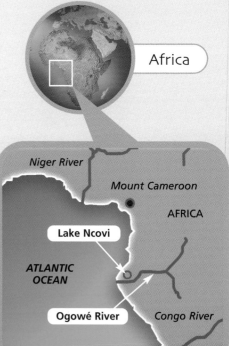

Africa

Niger River

Mount Cameroon

AFRICA

Lake Ncovi

ATLANTIC OCEAN

Ogowé River

Congo River

It was at Lake Ncovi that Mary first saw a group of gorillas. She later wrote, "I have seen many wild animals in their native wilds, but never have I seen anything to equal gorillas going through the bush; it is a graceful, powerful, superbly perfect hand-trapeze performance."

In Africa, Mary wore dresses with layers and layers of petticoats. When she fell fifteen feet into a game pit filled with sharp spikes, she lived to tell the story. "It is at these times you realize the blessing of a good, thick skirt," she said.

After being rescued from the game pit, Mary returned to her canoe. A hippopotamus was waiting, and "after scratching him behind the ear with my umbrella, we parted 'friends.'"

Traveling up the Ogowé River

Great Rivers of the World

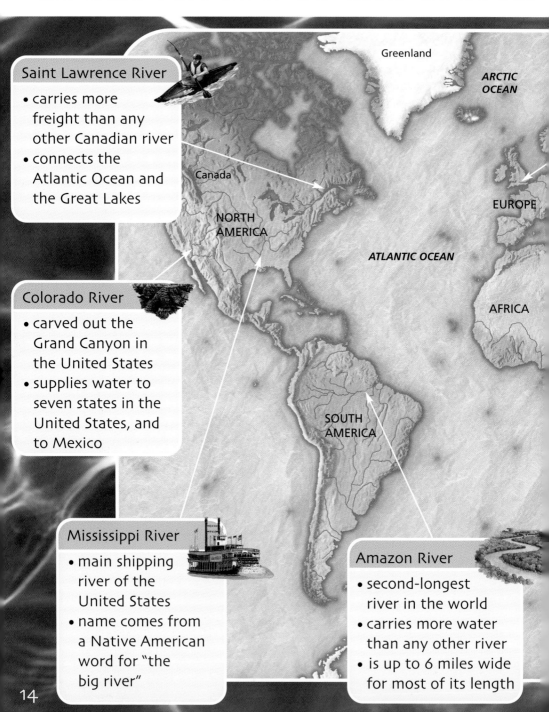

Saint Lawrence River

- carries more freight than any other Canadian river
- connects the Atlantic Ocean and the Great Lakes

Greenland

ARCTIC OCEAN

Canada

EUROPE

NORTH AMERICA

ATLANTIC OCEAN

AFRICA

Colorado River

- carved out the Grand Canyon in the United States
- supplies water to seven states in the United States, and to Mexico

SOUTH AMERICA

Mississippi River

- main shipping river of the United States
- name comes from a Native American word for "the big river"

Amazon River

- second-longest river in the world
- carries more water than any other river
- is up to 6 miles wide for most of its length

River Thames
- England's most important river
- flows through the heart of London past many famous buildings

Nile River

- longest river in the world
- was important for the Ancient Egyptians, and people still use it today

Yangtze River
- third-longest river in the world
- home to China's rare whitefin river dolphin

ASIA

China

India

PACIFIC OCEAN

INDIAN OCEAN

Murray River
- longest river in Australia
- necessary source of water for crops

AUSTRALIA

Zambezi River
- plunges over Victoria Falls
- is the border between two African countries

Ganges River

- India's longest river
- sacred to Hindu people
- forms the world's largest **delta**

A Tale of Two Rivers

The world's two largest rivers flow through very different land areas. The Nile is the longest river on Earth. It flows through the dry desert of northern Africa. The Amazon is the world's biggest river. It carries the most water and flows through a huge rain forest in South America.

The Nile River

Ancient Egyptians lived along the banks of the Nile and built great buildings such as graves and temples along its shores.
The people used the river for drinking and for **irrigating** their crops.

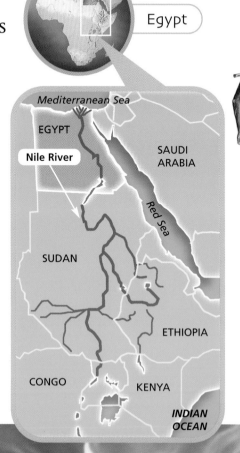

Egypt

Mediterranean Sea

EGYPT

Nile River

SAUDI ARABIA

Red Sea

SUDAN

ETHIOPIA

CONGO

KENYA

INDIAN OCEAN

Ancient Egyptians Farming the Shores of the Nile River

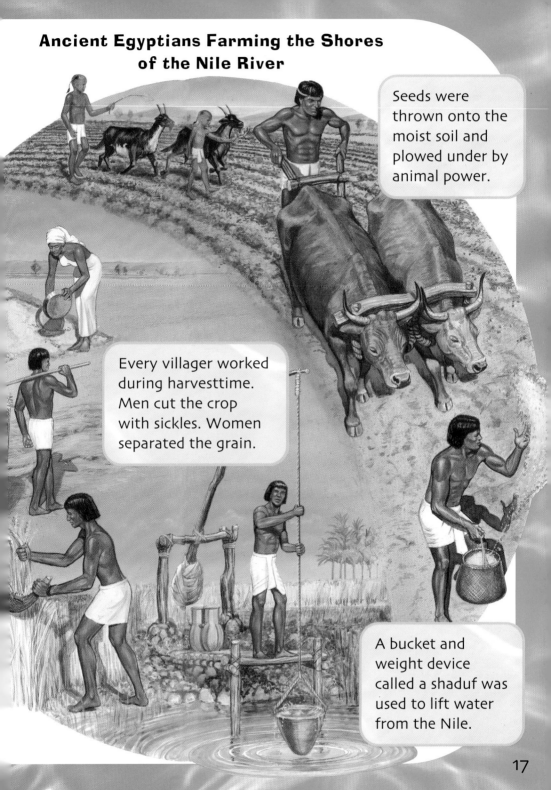

Seeds were thrown onto the moist soil and plowed under by animal power.

Every villager worked during harvesttime. Men cut the crop with sickles. Women separated the grain.

A bucket and weight device called a shaduf was used to lift water from the Nile.

The Amazon River

Many native groups live along the Amazon River. They fish in the wide river and hunt in the forest.

The Amazon is also home for an amazing variety of wildlife. There are over 2,000 kinds of fish in the Amazon river, including the flesh-eating piranha. The world's biggest snake, the anaconda, spends most of its life in the water. Some lily pads in the Amazon grow up to 3 feet wide. Each pad grows big and strong enough to hold the weight of a child.

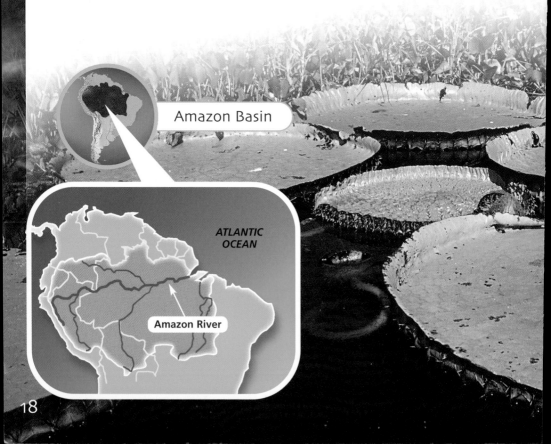

Amazon Basin

ATLANTIC
OCEAN

Amazon River

Piranha

WORD BUILDER

In 1541, Spanish explorer Francisco de Orellana traveled up the Amazon River. He said he was attacked by a band of women with bows and arrows. He called them Amazons, like the fierce female warriors of Greek legend. This was how the river got its name.

Life Along a River

The Mississippi, together with its main tributary the Missouri, forms the greatest river system in North America. For centuries, the river was an important trading route for Native Americans. Later, it was the pathway for European settlement in the United States. From the early 1800s, steamboats took settlers and goods up and down the river.

The Mississippi curls through hills down to the plains and **bayous** of the South. Many people have settled along its banks, creating an exciting mix of groups and ways of life.

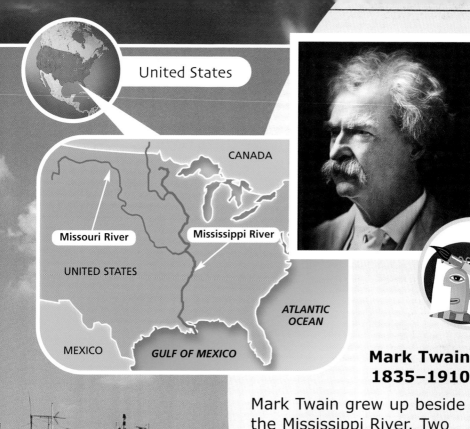

United States

CANADA

Missouri River

Mississippi River

UNITED STATES

ATLANTIC
OCEAN

MEXICO

GULF OF MEXICO

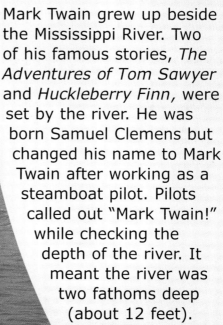

Mark Twain
1835–1910

Mark Twain grew up beside the Mississippi River. Two of his famous stories, *The Adventures of Tom Sawyer* and *Huckleberry Finn,* were set by the river. He was born Samuel Clemens but changed his name to Mark Twain after working as a steamboat pilot. Pilots called out "Mark Twain!" while checking the depth of the river. It meant the river was two fathoms deep (about 12 feet).

Using Rivers Today

Many towns and cities around the world get their water supply directly from rivers. As well as drinking, cooking, and washing with it, people use river water to manufacture goods and produce electricity.

Some factories need huge amounts of water for cleaning and mixing with products. If they use river water to flush away waste materials, it can cause river pollution.

Even with today's many roads and rails, rivers are still used to transport goods. Tugs and barges move heavy freight cheaply and quickly. In the countryside, farmers channel river water into ditches, canals, and sprinklers to irrigate their fields. In some cities, people live on rivers in houseboats.

A houseboat on a river is home to many people in cities around the world.

Power from a River

In the past, people used the power of running water in fast-flowing rivers to turn waterwheels. Waterwheels powered simple machines such as grinders and hammers.

Now we use rivers to make electricity by turning huge waterwheels called turbines. A dam is built across a river to hold back the water. When the dam gates are opened, water rushes through a tunnel and hits the turbines. The force of the water spins the turbines to make electricity. This is called **hydroelectric power.**

Hydroelectric power is clean and cheap to produce. However, taking care to protect the land, the plants, and the animals that live beside the river is important when building a dam.

The Clutha River in New Zealand before the Clyde Dam was built

The completed Clyde Dam

Change with Care

People have used and changed rivers for hundreds of years. They've built dams and banks to stop flooding. They've built canals and **aqueducts** to move water. They've straightened rivers and built **locks** to help transport goods. They've even drained rivers to provide more land.

People have also changed rivers by polluting them. Today, people in many places are learning that it is important to care for rivers.

River Thames, England

Cleaning the Connecticut

The Connecticut River was once the most polluted river in the United States. Some parts ran red with dyes from factories. In 1972, people began river cleanups. Now, salmon are returning, and the river is clean and beautiful again.

SITESEEING · WATER, EARTH, & SKY ·

What can we do to look after rivers?

Visit www.rigbyinfoquest.com
for more about **RIVERS.**

Fun on the River

Rivers are also fun! People enjoy swimming and fishing from the banks of rivers. Some people row, sail, or cruise along slow-moving rivers. Others take on fast-flowing rivers by "shooting the rapids" in boats and rafts.

Rivers are often beautiful places to visit for a walk, a picnic, or seeing wildlife. Some have awesome features such as plunging waterfalls and white-water rapids.

A slow-moving river is an ideal place for teaching children how to paddle a canoe.

Which River Is Safe?

Rivers are graded on a scale of 1 to 6. Grade 1 rivers have little or no current and no big rocks or holes. Grade 6 rivers are very dangerous, with large drops over waterfalls and huge boulders. They are usually thought to be impossible for any activity, or "unrunnable," even by experts.

Glossary

aqueduct – a pipe or a channel built for moving water across long distances

bayou – a word used mainly in the southern United States to describe a stream that runs through wet, marshy areas. It runs from or into a larger river or a lake.

delta – an area of land built out into a sea or a lake. A delta forms a fan shape where the flow of a river stops and mud, sand, or eroded rock are dropped.

hydroelectric power – power that is produced by the force of running water

irrigating – bringing water to the land by using special pipes, sprinklers, and ditches. In some areas where there is little rain, farmers use the water from nearby rivers to irrigate their fields.

lock – an enclosed part of a river with gates built at each end so boats can be lifted or lowered to different sections of the river

mouth – the place where a river enters a sea or a lake

rapids - parts of a river where the water flows very quickly over rocks

source – the beginning of a stream or a river

tributary – a stream or a river that flows into a larger river

Index

Africa 12–17

Amazon River 14, 16, 18–19

Cartier, Jacques 11

Colorado River 14

Connecticut River 27

de Orellana, Francisco 19

fish, river 8–9, 18–19

Ganges River 5, 15

hydroelectric power 24–25

Kingsley, Mary 12–13

Mississippi River 14, 20–21

Murray River 15

Nile River 15–17

Ogowé River 12–13

plants, river 8, 18

pollution 22, 26–27

River Thames 15, 26–27

Saint Lawrence River 10–11, 14

waterfalls 7, 28–29

Yangtze River 15

Zambezi River 15

Discussion Starters

1 Many explorers followed rivers when they explored unknown lands. Why do you think it was helpful to follow a river? What does a river have that would have helped these explorers on their journeys?

2 White-water rafting is an exciting river sport. What other sports can you think of that take place on a river? Are there any Olympic events raced on a river?

3 In some parts of the world, rivers freeze during the winter months. Skating on a frozen river is fun, but it is more dangerous than skating on an indoor ice rink. Why? What do you need to consider to make sure you skate safely on a frozen river?